MYSTERIOUS DOUBLES:
The Story of Twins

By Liz Bowden
Illustrated by Gerald E. Smith

Copyright© 1979 by Contemporary Perspectives, Inc.
All rights reserved. No part of this book may be reproduced or utilized in any form or by any means, electronic or mechanical, or by any information storage and retrieval system, without permission in writing from the Publisher. Inquiries should be addressed to the PUBLISHER: Contemporary Perspectives, Inc., 223 East 48th Street, New York, New York 10017.

This book is distributed by Silver Burdett Company, Morristown, New Jersey 07960.

Library of Congress Number: 79-19034

Cover photo courtesy of Ira M. Adler.
Photos on pages 26, 29, 31, and 43, UPI.
Photo on page 35, S. Olan.
Photo on page 37, courtesy of Ira M. Adler.
Photo on page 41, The Granger Collection, New York.

Every effort has been made to trace the ownership of all copyrighted material in this book and to obtain permission for its use.

Library of Congress Cataloging in Publication Data

Bowden, Liz, 1928-
  Mysterious doubles, the story of twins.

  SUMMARY: Focuses on the special closeness shared by twins and discusses the development of identical, fraternal, mirror-image, and Siamese twins.
  1. Twins — Psychology — Juvenile literature. 2. Twins — Juvenile literature. [1. Twins] I. Title.
BF 723.T9B62   155.9'2'4   79-19034
ISBN 0-89547-080-2

Manufactured in the United States of America
ISBN 0-89547-080-2

Contents

Chapter 1
  A Strange Portrait   5

Chapter 2
  Special People   20

Chapter 3
  What Are Twins?   34

Chapter 4
  Twin Fun   45

Chapter 1

A Strange Portrait

"This is no day to stay in bed," Jud thought. The first rays of sunshine peeped over the flat Nebraska cornfields. By the time they bent their way into Jud's bedroom, he was dressed.

Jud ran downstairs into the big farm kitchen and gulped his breakfast. His mother watched and smiled.

"What's the big rush, Jud?"

"The fair! Today's the county fair. Don't tell me you forgot!" Jud could not believe that anybody alive could forget about the fair.

Jud's mother had not really forgotten. She was teasing. She knew how important the county fair was to a twelve-year-old. But she wanted to hear the excitement in her son's voice as he told her why he was in such a hurry.

Now she smiled. "Jud, I want you to have fun today." Then she said, almost sternly, "But I want you to be careful spending your money." That said, she kissed him and pressed a shiny half-dollar into his hand.

"Wow! Thanks, Mom!" In those days, a half-dollar was a lot of money — more than Jud had ever had to spend. He gave his mother a hug and promised he'd be back by dinner time. Then he ran out of the house, clutching his silver half-dollar.

A moment later, he returned and stuck his head inside the screen door to the kitchen. "Hey, Mom!" he called, "I love ya!" And he ran off again without hearing her reply.

The year was 1932. It was the time of the Great Depression. Practically the entire country was poor. But as Jud ran along the dusty road between knee-high cornfields, he wasn't thinking about the holes in his sneakers. He didn't care about the patches on his overalls, or the nights he went to bed hungry. He was thinking only about how he'd spend his half-dollar at the fair.

When Jud arrived at the fairgrounds, he walked slowly from booth to booth and ride to ride. He wanted to take a careful look at everything. Later he would decide where to spend his fifty cents. He was walking and looking over his shoulder, when ... smash! He bumped right into another boy. Both of them fell down.

"Hey, I'm sorry," said Jud, brushing himself off.

"My fault," said the other boy. When Jud looked up he couldn't believe his eyes. Was he looking into a mirror?

Jud was dressed in worn country overalls. The other boy had on fancy city clothes. Even so, the two looked *exactly alike!* They could have been brothers. More than that, they could have been twins!

And Jud said so. "We look like twins!" he blurted out.

The other boy was just as amazed. "Golly, you're right!" he said. "We have to be twins! We even *sound* like each other!"

"My name's Jud."

"Mine's Harry."

"I ... I ... came from the orphanage. Did you too?" Jud asked shyly.

Harry didn't answer right away. He just looked straight at Jud for a moment. Then, slowly, he nodded

his head. Then his eyes brightened and he grinned. "We *must* be twins. Let's tell our folks we found each other!"

At first Jud wasn't sure. Then he grinned too. "Okay," he said, "but not yet. Not until dinner time. Come on, let's have some fun first. Then we'll surprise them."

Both boys had the most wonderful day of their lives. Harry had five dollars. Jud said it was too much to share. Harry threatened to tear it up if they didn't go fifty-fifty, and so they spent it all.

They rode every ride. They ate hot dogs and ice cream until their stomachs ached. They ran and laughed and told stories about themselves. Jud never felt so close to another person in his life. It was almost as if Harry was his other half.

And the most amazing thing was that they seemed to read each other's minds! One would start a sentence. The other would finish it. One would start a story, and the other would end it. Finding a brother was great, but finding a twin brother — who even knew what you were *thinking* . . . . That was almost unbelievable!

"Harry!" It was a woman's voice — sharp, shrill, and frightened. She was well dressed and looked nervous. She glanced from Harry to Jud and back again to Harry. "We've been looking for you all afternoon!"

"Mother," said Harry excitedly, "this is Jud, my twin brother!"

Harry's mother looked stunned. She grabbed Harry by the arm and quickly led him away. "Now that's the most ridiculous thing I ever heard," Jud heard her say, as she and Harry disappeared into the crowd.

A few moments later, Jud heard Harry call, "See you later, Jud!" But he could no longer see him.

The happiest day of Jud's young life suddenly turned into the saddest. The closeness he felt with Harry was gone. In its place was a strange emptiness Jud had never known before. All at once, Jud felt very much alone.

Jud went on home. He looked so sad that evening that his parents thought he was sick — perhaps from drinking too many sodas. But when he finally spoke, they found that something was puzzling him.

"Mom ... Dad," he asked very quietly, "do I have a twin brother?"

Jud's parents looked at each other and then back to Jud. He knew the answer even before they spoke. Yes, he did have a twin brother at the orphanage. As much as they wanted to adopt both boys, they just couldn't afford to raise two children. Besides, there were some rich folks from the city who wanted very much to take the other boy.

Jud was excited all over again. "I *saw* him today! I *met* him! His name is Harry, and we were together all day at the fair. Can I go see him? Please?"

Once again, Jud knew what the answer would be. This time it was no.

"They're rich city folks, Jud. You wouldn't be welcome."

Jud walked slowly up to his room.

In October 1942, Jud was at the opposite end of the world. World War II was being fought. Jud was with the marines on Guadalcanal, an island in the South Pacific. A fierce battle was raging. The marines were defending their airstrip, and the army had just landed. The enemy was pounding the island, and Jud had taken cover in a foxhole.

As the battle roared on, a flare sizzled overhead and lit up the night with an eerie red glow. Had the flare not gone off at that moment, Jud would never have recognized the soldier who jumped into the foxhole beside him. It was his twin brother Harry.

"Well, look who's here," said Harry with a big grin. "My double."

Double, thought Jud. Harry didn't call him his twin, but his double. Had Harry's parents not told him the truth?

Even though he didn't know they were twins, Harry was delighted to see Jud once again. Jud, of course, was thrilled. In their foxhole, the two forgot about the shells exploding all around them. They talked through the night and caught up on each other's lives.

Jud had dreamed of this moment for ten years. Yet, now that he was listening to Harry, he was suddenly disappointed. Their lives were so different. Harry was married. He had gone to college. Jud had never been to college. Compared to Harry, he felt uneducated. Jud was just a marine private. Harry was an army captain. He wanted so much to tell Harry that they were really twin brothers. But he could not. Sadly, he felt Harry would not have been proud to be his brother.

Harry insisted they exchange addresses and keep in touch. They promised each other to be sure to get together once the war was over. Early the next morning, when the fighting stopped, Harry slipped out of the foxhole. He had to get his troops back together.

That same day, Jud's unit was moved to another area.

The brothers did not hear from each other for nearly three more years, until April 1945. The long war was still going on. This time, the island was Okinawa.

Jud was fighting in a mighty battle. Suddenly, over the thunder of bombs and shellfire, he heard the moans of a man in pain. Was it an enemy trap? Was it a trick to lure him from safety? Jud had to be careful. He slipped his bayonet between his teeth. Rifle at the ready, he crawled carefully along the battlefield toward the sounds.

He reached the wounded soldier who was huddled in a heap. It was his brother Harry!

"Don't worry, Harry," said Jud softly. "I'm going back for help."

"That's you, isn't it, Jud?" moaned Harry. He seemed to know, even through his pain.

"Yeah, your double, Jud."

"Don't go, Jud. Don't leave me here. I'm hit bad. I don't think I can make it much longer. Just stay with me these last few minutes."

The sound of gunfire was deafening. Harry's words could barely be heard as he struggled to breathe. Jud held his brother in his arms and tried to crawl back to safety. Harry was mumbling something about a message to his wife, but Jud couldn't hear it.

"Jud. Stop a minute." Harry whispered with all his

remaining strength. "I gotta tell you something really strange. You know what I wish, Jud? I've wished it ever since ... we met at the fair. I've always wished ... we were brothers. You know? Twins ...." He tried to say more. Then his head dropped, and he was quiet.

"We are, Harry, we are!" Jud shook his brother, trying to make him hear. "We're brothers, we're twins! I've known it all along." Jud began to cry softly. "I wanted to tell you on Guadalcanal, but I was afraid. I thought we were too far apart. You went to college. You got to be an officer. It seems foolish now, but it didn't then ...." Jud continued talking as Harry's body lay in his arms. But Harry was no longer breathing. Jud's words were lost in the sounds of battle.

A few months later the war ended. Jud was sent back to a base in California. One evening he went to the U.S.O. club. Kay Olsen, a local artist, talked the sad-faced Jud into letting her sketch his portrait.

She tried to get him to smile as she sketched, but he couldn't. Jud hadn't smiled since Harry was killed.

When Kay finished her portrait, she showed it to Jud. He was dumbfounded. What Kay had drawn was not a sad-faced soldier, but a smiling one. And strangest of all, she had not drawn a marine — but an army captain!

"Don't change it! Don't change it!" cried Jud, seeing his brother in the sketch. "You didn't draw me. You drew Harry! You drew my twin brother! See, he's even smiling! He was always smiling."

Now Kay Olsen found herself just as amazed as Jud. Why, she wondered, had she drawn the picture this way? The face was Jud's. But in the picture he was smiling and wearing a captain's uniform. She didn't understand. A friend of hers, Dr. Arthur Trevenning Harris, was sitting nearby. She showed him the picture and pointed out Jud across the room.

Dr. Harris looked first at the picture, then at Jud and back to the picture again. Then he went over to Jud's table and said, "You must have a twin!"

"I did." Jud slumped in his chair. Tears came to his eyes although he tried to hold them back. "My brother was killed on Okinawa." Now Jud turned to Kay. "But I never told *you* I had a twin brother who was a captain in the army! Yet that's who you've drawn. You drew my twin brother!"

Jud told Kay and Dr. Harris the whole story. Somehow it felt good, talking about his brother again. Jud told them how he had met Harry at the county fair. He told the whole story, right to their last battle on Okinawa. He told of how he wanted Harry to know they were twins, but never could tell him. Until it was too late. "I've been miserable ever since."

Dr. Harris put his hand on Jud's shoulder. "Jud," he said softly, "you of all people should know that twins are different from other people. They're close to each other — in many ways that are still mysterious. Why do you think that when Kay looked at you, she saw Harry?"

Jud looked up at the doctor. "You think — is it possible? Could *he* have told her? Is this Harry's way of telling me he knows we are twins?"

"Who knows?" said Dr. Harris. "But Kay had no way of knowing your twin was in the army or that he was a captain. Somehow she 'saw.' Maybe Harry guided her hand, Jud. Maybe he did get your message. Maybe this is his way of telling you."

This story is true. It has been related more recently by the doctor's son, Derek T. Harris, of Newport Beach, California. His wife and stepmother also went over to Jud's table in the U.S.O. club after the picture of Jud's twin brother was drawn.

Can twins really be *that* close?

Let's try to find out.

Chapter 2

Special People

Roger Brooks and Tony Milasi were identical twins who were separated at birth. They found each other 24 years later. They were brought together when a friend of Tony's saw Roger in a Florida restaurant. The friend could hardly believe his eyes. Roger looked so much like Tony. In fact, he thought at first that Roger *was* Tony. When the twins finally met for the first time, they too were amazed. It wasn't just that they looked so much alike. It was as if they had lived the same life!

The twins had grown up a thousand miles apart. They were raised by very different types of parents. Each had been told his twin brother had died. Yet

each often had a dream — that his brother was passing in the opposite direction in an airplane or a speeding train. Both had always been sure they would meet some day!

When they finally did, they found that they were very much alike even though they had grown up so far apart — and in such different ways. They used the same after-shave lotion, and even the same toothpaste — although it was a little-known Swedish brand! Both had had problems with their lower right wisdom teeth, and they had scars of the same shape on their left arms. When they were tested, their IQs were just one point apart. Both took personality tests. Separately, they had to answer hundreds of questions. When the answers were read, it was as if only one of them had taken both tests!

Of course, two people can have the same IQ or the same wisdom tooth troubles. Any two people might use the same little-known toothpaste. And the same family can be alike in all sorts of ways. But how can the twins' personality tests be explained?

Scientists still cannot answer such questions, even about twins who grow up together. But questions like these become even greater mysteries when they are asked about twins who have been separated from birth. How is it that they so often have the same habits? Why do so many like and dislike the same foods, the same clothes, the same books, the same movies?

Is it possible that in some strange way, twins are really two halves of the same person?

Roger and Tony had missed a lot of the fun of growing up together. But now they had found each other. They started making up for the fun they should have had as twins. Shortly after they met they saw a sign in the window of a restaurant. "All the spaghetti you can eat — $1.00." They quickly worked out a plan.

Roger went in, sat down, and ordered a plate of spaghetti. And then another. And then another. The twins were both big men. And they both loved spaghetti.

When Roger finished his third heaping plate of spaghetti, he told the amazed waitress that he was going to put some money in the parking meter, and he'd be right back.

And back came hungry Tony! He was dressed exactly like Roger. There was no way you could tell them apart. After one plate, the manager came out to watch. After two plates, the cook came out to watch.

And after three plates, Roger walked back into the restaurant to greet Tony. Everybody enjoyed the joke.

When last heard from, Roger and Tony were still together — not only brothers, not only neighbors, but partners in the Twin Market in Binghamton, New York.

In 1979 James Lewis and James Springer, separated since they were five weeks old, met again after 34 years. "It isn't like meeting a stranger," said Lewis. "Part of my life has now come together. I'll start to say something and he'll finish it. It's as if he can read my mind."

The twins are the same size and weight, and they look and behave alike. They enjoy many of the same things.

Before they met, each of them had been a policeman, and they both married and divorced women named Linda. Was it all a coincidence?

Scientists are very excited by the Lewis-Springer

James Lewis and James Springer — twins whose lives were mirror images although they lived apart for 34 years.

get-together. The twins are now being tested at the University of Minnesota. The test results may help to answer an old and mysterious question: What is more important in making human beings act the way they do? Is it heredity — the *genes* we get from our parents at birth? Eye and hair color, along with many other conditions of health and appearance, come to us through genes — the chemical bodies we inherit from our parents. Or are we more affected by our *environment* — the places we grow up in, the people we are close to, and the surroundings in which we are raised?

Identical twins receive the same genes from their parents. So the only difference between them should come from their environment. But are the answers that simple? James Lewis and James Springer grew up in different places. Yet they grew up to be very much alike.

Whatever the reason, we do know that there are unexplained ways in which twins seem to be very much like each other. The records of Dick and Tom Van Arsdale, the only twins ever to play in the National Basketball Association, are almost exactly alike. It's almost as if it were the same person playing twice! After 12 years, here are the look-alike totals of these look-alike basketball stars:

	Dick	Tom
Games played	921	929
Field goals made	5,431	5,505
Field goals attempted	11,661	12,763
Total points	15,079	14,232
Av. pts./game	16.4	15.3
Rebounds	3,807	3,948

Many stories are told about the strange ways in which certain twins can read each other's minds. One story tells of twins who could divide their studying time. One would go to school one day, and the other the next. They would take turns studying every other day. Yet each of them passed the tests!

Professor H.H. Newman of the University of Chicago claims to have discovered a pair of twins who divided their textbooks into equal piles when they

Dick and Tom Van Arsdale, the only twins ever to play in the National Basketball Association, are more than look-alikes. Their playing records are almost identical.

were studying for tests. Each twin would study one pile, but not the other. Mysteriously, when they took their tests both did equally well on all subjects. Could each twin have somehow "picked up" the information that was in the other twin's mind?

Whether or not some twins can actually read each other's minds, we do know that they understand each other's minds so well that they can use their own special language! That's what happened with nine-year-old twins Ginny and Gracy Kennedy of Columbus, Georgia.

"Cabengo padem manibadu peetu," Gracy says.

"Soan nee bad tangkmatt," replies Ginny.

Nobody else in the world but Ginny and Gracy knows what these strange sounds mean. It's their own private code. But if a secret language seems to be a dream come true, it was more like a nightmare for Ginny and Gracy's parents when the two girls were seven years old. For some reason, neither of the twins could speak or understand a word of English, and they had to be kept out of school. *Yet they understood each other perfectly!*

Today, Ginny and Gracy do attend school. They are in separate classes to encourage them to meet and talk with other children. Now they will learn to speak a real language. And at the same time, experts are studying the "language" the twins made up — completely on

Ginny and Gracy Kennedy are twins who speak a language only they can understand.

their own! Scientists hope that Ginny and Gracy's special skill with their own "code" may help solve some of the mysteries of how the earliest human beings learned to speak to each other.

Mr. and Mrs. Burl Wolf of Bosier City, Louisiana, had five-year-old twin girls. They looked so much alike that when the time came to enroll them at school, they had to check the footprints on their birth certificates to tell them apart. This was because the girls loved to confuse people. Each of them insisted she was the other!

For a short time the Wolfs were given some help in telling the twins apart. A mole appeared on the forehead of one of the girls. But soon, a mole appeared in exactly the same place on the forehead of the other sister! Mysteriously, the moles popped up three more times. As soon as one sister would get a mole, it was just a matter of days or weeks before the other grew one in the very same spot!

Many of the strange things that happen to twins can't yet be explained. But, of course, there is much that scientists *do* know about these mysterious and fascinating doubles.

Chapter 3

What Are Twins?

The word "twin" comes from an ancient Anglo-Saxon word meaning "two strands twisted together." Today, even with all our scientific knowledge, many mysteries about twins are far from being untwisted.

Twins are most often born minutes apart. But sometimes one might be born hours or even days after the other. Few mothers give birth to twins. One pair of twins comes in about every 86 births.

Twins are either fraternal or identical. Fraternal twins might be called "two-egg" twins. They come from two different eggs, each of which may carry a different heredity (different genes). So the eye and

Doctors Monroe and Richard Gliedman are fraternal twins whose lives bear striking similarities. Both are orthodontists and Professors of Dentistry.

Meridith and Joshua Lew are just like any other sister and brother. They each came from a separate egg cell, but they were born together. They are *fraternal* twins.

hair color of fraternal twins, and such things as their size, shape, and intelligence, might be quite different.

Fraternal comes from the Latin word *frater*, meaning "brother." And that's just what two-egg twins are like — ordinary brothers or sisters. They might look very much alike ... or quite different. They can even be of different sexes.

Identical twins, however, come from only one egg. For some unknown reason the egg splits into two parts. The sooner the egg splits in the mother's body, the more the twins will look alike. One-egg twins inherit the same genes. Hair and eye color and other hereditary traits are the same. And they are always of the same sex.

Any pair of twins may look almost exactly alike, but that doesn't always mean that they're identical. Sometimes it's very hard to find out.

Some years ago, a *skin-graft test* was the exciting proof that solved a very unusual "which-is-which?" twin mystery.

The story began in 1941, in a hospital in the Swiss town of Fribourg. Two mothers had just given birth — one to twin boys, and the other to a single boy. When they left the hospital, Mrs. Joye, the mother of the

Identical twins Jill and Leslie Adler not only look alike, they seem to feel the same way about many things.

twins, went home with Paul and Philippe. Mrs. Vatter took her infant son Ernst.

As the Joye twins grew up, they differed in many ways, so everyone thought they must be fraternal twins coming from two eggs.

But things began to look mysterious when the twins were six years old and went to the same school with Ernst Vatter. Even though Paul and Philippe were "twins," Philippe looked *exactly* like Ernst — who wasn't even related to him!

You can probably guess the rest. The parents thought there must have been a baby mix-up at the hospital, so they had a skin-graft test made. And sure enough, Philippe and Ernst were identical twins!

Since identical twins come from one egg and have the same hereditary factors, it's possible to take skin from one twin and graft, or join, it to the other twin. It's just as if you put a piece of skin from one part of your body onto another.

But if you try this with two people who aren't related — or even with fraternal twins — the grafted skin will not last.

Sometimes nature plays even stranger tricks on identical twins. The twins may fail to separate

completely while they're still in their mother's womb. Somehow their bodies remain joined. Still attached to each other, they are born as "Siamese" twins. It happens rarely — perhaps 1 in 250,000 live births.

Chang and Eng (which mean "left" and "right") were the most famous Siamese twins. But Chang and Eng were not Siamese. They were only born in Siam to parents who were Chinese. But from that time on, twins born attached to each other have been called "Siamese."

Chang and Eng were joined at the breastbone by a band of flesh about three and a half inches long and eight inches around. The band could be stretched so they could stand or lie down back to back. Chang was one inch shorter than Eng and wore special shoes to make up the difference in height. Both twins were good athletes and enjoyed swimming, diving, and climbing.

Eventually they were seen by the public as "freaks" in the circus of the famous showman P.T. Barnum. Unfortunately, the stories Barnum told the world about the twins could easily have been stretching the truth.

One such story says a British merchant first found Chang and Eng when they were 13 years old. He rescued them just as they were about to be put to

Chang and Eng were famous Siamese twins who were joined at the breastbone.

death. They were thought to be a bad omen. Another story tells of an American sea captain who smuggled the twins out of Siam. He knew he could make a lot of money by selling them to the circus. In any event, with P.T. Barnum's publicity the Siamese twins soon became world famous.

With their fame came fortune. When they were 30, they decided to settle down in the quiet farming town of Mt. Airy, North Carolina. Two years later, in one of the strangest wedding ceremonies ever performed, Chang and Eng married two sisters.

The entire world wondered how such a marriage could ever last. But Chang and Eng worked out special living arrangements. The two families lived in different houses, and moved back and forth between them.

Over the years, the two couples had 22 children. There were no Siamese twins among them. There are now more than a thousand descendents of the famous twins. The family took on a new name, Bunker. Among their relatives are a former president of the Union Pacific Railway and a major general in the United States Army.

Stories say that it was impossible to talk with just one of the twins. Chang and Eng would finish each other's sentences. Each claimed he could read his twin's thoughts. That's why they could never play checkers with each other. They loved the game. But it was not much fun knowing what move the other twin would make even before he made it!

Unhappily, the twins were never able to have what they wanted more than anything else — to have their

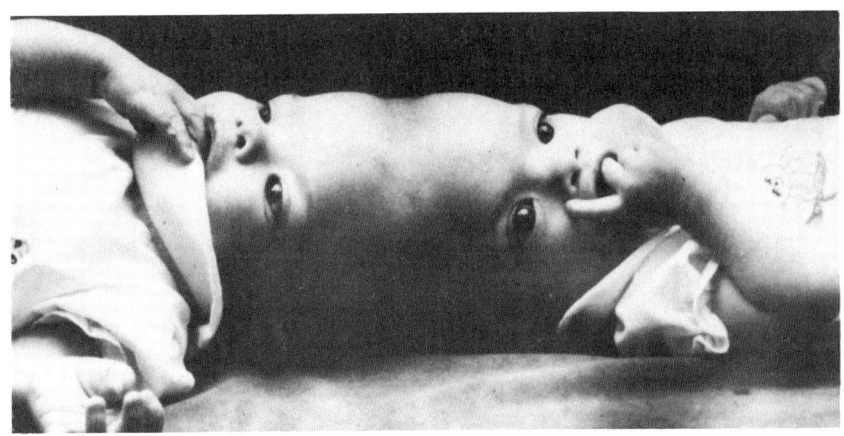

The Hansen twins, Elisa and Lisa, were born attached at the tops of their heads. Salt Lake City doctors separated the girls in 1979. They are shown (bottom) with father, mother, and baby sister.

bodies separated. They visited doctor after doctor, but they could find no one who knew a way to do it.

In January 1894, Chang became very ill. Eng woke up one morning to find Chang dead beside him. The family ran to find a doctor. This time an operation was not a matter of choice. It would be to separate the living from the dead.

But before the doctor could get there, Eng had died of fright.

Fortunately, times have changed. Although Siamese twins are still rare enough to be front-page news when they are born, they are usually separated safely when they're very young.

Chapter 4

Twin Fun

One of the nicest true tales about twin mischief is told about Jean and Auguste Piccard, the famous Swiss scientists who made record balloon flights and deep-sea explorations. One day, Jean Piccard went to a barber for a shave, and complained: "Shaves just aren't what they used to be."

"What do you mean?" asked the barber, feeling insulted.

"Well," sighed Jean, "something's happening. I don't know if it's the bad blades or the bad barbers — but whenever I get a shave now, I need another in just a few hours."

"Monsieur!" exclaimed the barber. "I will give you a shave that will last all day, I promise!"

"They all say that," sighed Jean.

"Monsieur, if you need a shave before tomorrow, I will personally give you another one free. How's that?"

"Fair enough," said Jean.

The barber shaved Jean, who then left.

A couple of hours later, Jean's identical twin, Auguste, entered the same barber shop. He was dressed exactly as Jean had been dressed, but he had a full beard!

"See?" announced Auguste to the astonished barber. "What did I tell you?"

So Auguste received a free shave. But to this day, the barber can't understand what happened!

What is it like to be a twin? It can be just like having an ordinary brother or sister, or it can mean you have a friend closer than any other — maybe close enough to read his or her thoughts! You may share likes and dislikes, habits, professions, even a secret language. Twins can have fun confusing their parents, friends, and teachers

about who's who. If you know twins who are also practical jokers, watch out!

Many mysteries about twins remain unsolved. We know that twins share a special bond. But no one can explain the claim of many twins that they can pick up each other's thoughts and feelings, even over great distances. Can such a bond be scientifically proved? Can the mysteries of twins' secret language be unraveled? And how can we explain the amazing similarities between twins who grow up separately?

These questions are being studied by scientists and doctors. Until they are answered, twins remain mysterious doubles.